healing
is my
hustle

RISE BOOKS AND COFFEE

ISBN: 9798218130800

Printed in the United States of America

Donielle's products are available at special discounts with bulk edu-
cational, fundraising, or business purchases. For information about
special discounts, or to book Donielle for an event, please submit
inquiries via www.DonielleElizabeth.com.

Concept By: Donielle Elizabeth
@Donielle_Elizabeth | www.DonielleElizabeth.com

*Dedicated to the Black girls
who bleed in silence.
May you find rest and healing.*

Table of Contents

lived
experiences

Myths

They assume Black girls are
pliable because we bend and they never see us break,
impenetrable because our self-harm scars don't leave an
obvious mark,
superhuman because our trauma is painted on the canvas of
a smiling face.

The truth is we bleed internally,
and one day we pass out
from all the hemorrhaging
alone.

The myths can't save us from what we carry.

Halloween

Regular Black girls
don't celebrate Halloween
because we wear costumes
and masks all year round.

We learned early in life,
there's no need to
celebrate what's normal.

Skin

They say Black girl skin is
the toughest of them all,
the most unlikely of any mount,
the rarest of any hide,
and still, black girl skin is the most
vulnerable of any species,
categorically undervalued,
predictably overlooked.

Angry

Angry is what they call us when their tongues are too remedial to articulate our pain.

Competitors

They compare and contrast,
tick and tie,
hoping we turn against each other,
so at our own hands,
we die.

strong black
woman

Weak

She was a strong black woman,
built like no epidural needed,
did it all by herself,
poured from an empty cup,
squeezed her body to the last drop,
filled her plate to the brim,
never took time to replenish.

Three side hustles and a main job,
maintained consistent service with two signal bars,
grinded through it all with no self-care breaks,
freed, but work ethic in the aroma of slavery,
product of the unbreakable variety,
carried the burden of strength,
with no complaints,
upheld society's unrealistic expectations.

Until one day, her heart broke without warning,
and she died of self-neglect.
At her funeral,
they called her strong,
but strength is no compliment,
if it only leaves you weak in the end.

Aunties

We've seen our aunties lose siblings, spouses, and children.

They never cry, and for this,
we always call them strong
because we can't admit that they're numb.

Their bodies don't have use for emotions
because they've scoured the entire range,
but there's no language
that could ever explain the depths of their pain.

Caution

Be wary of the ones who call you strong. They call you strong
to tell you they don't want to be you. Without telling you,
they don't want to be you.

Fallacy

Our foremothers passed the legacy of trauma,
and to compensate,
they groomed us for strength to be the lovers of our life.

Taught us the greatest fallacy of them all,
that we could depend on strength
to keep us warm when life let us down.

But in time, we'd learn strength was an unfaithful lover too.

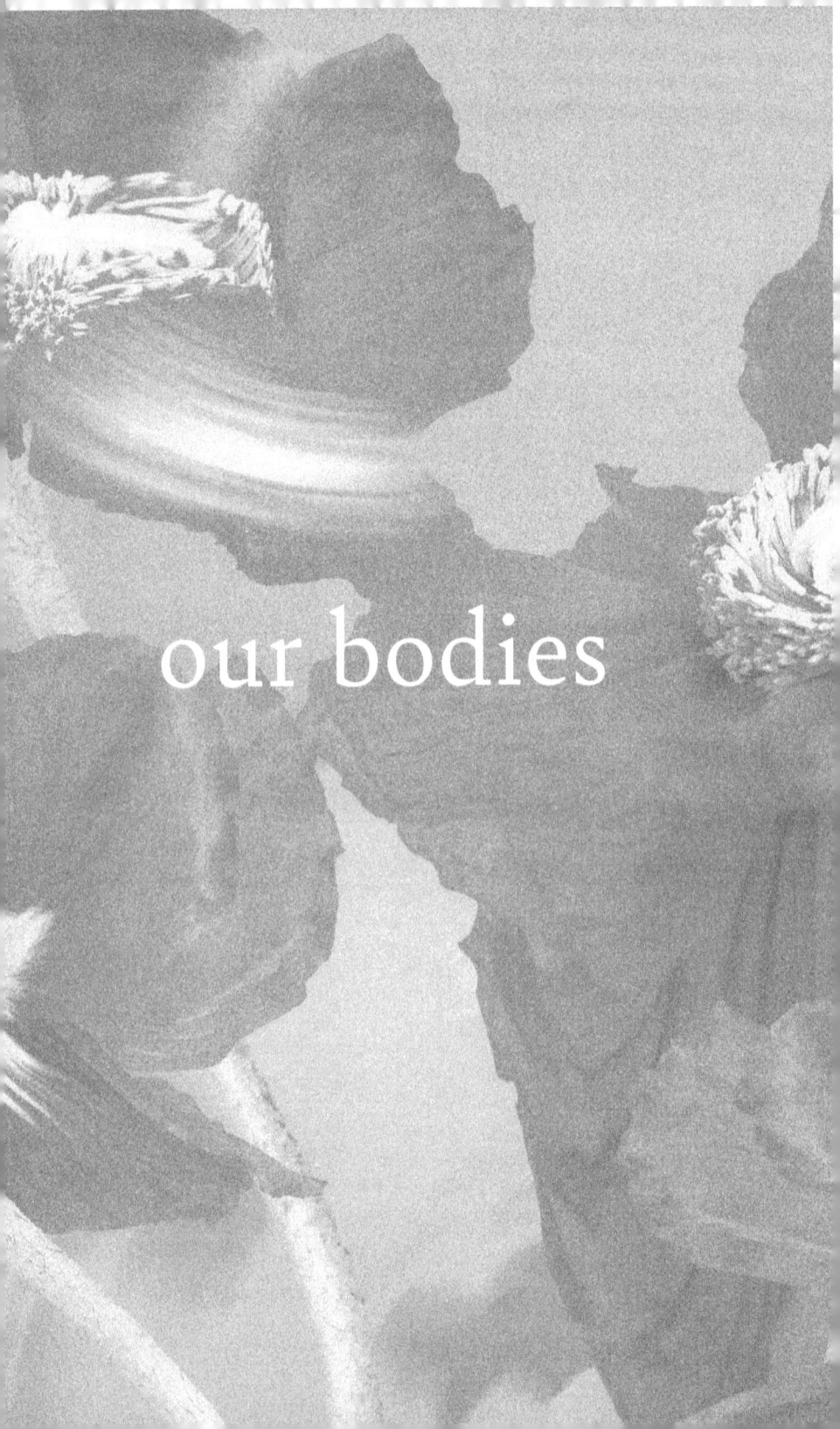

our bodies

Heavy

Mainstream can't take it when they see your heavy.

When your heavy is a reflection of how good their ancestors ate off your oppression.

When you exercise your right to take up space, and your bones are too big to shrink down to the size of their comparisons.

When they attempt to body shame you, but instead, your confidence serves the shame on their plate.

When you work out that your beauty isn't dependent on eurocentric scales, and your artistry expands well beyond the confines of their ideal dress size.

When you become uncomfortable with the lies they feed you, so you sustain yourself on the comfort of your own power.

When they pressure you to downsize,
but you decide to embrace your body mass
because it reminds you of the peace you gained when you
freed yourself.

Family Gatherings

At the dinner table,
we never outed the uncles who touched us,
we swallowed pieces of our soul in between soul food,
we broke bread over broken boundaries,
and we washed down the bitter taste of shame,
but we never outed the uncles who touched us.

We were little girls too powerless to disrupt dinner for truth,
too afraid to gather family over abuse.

Now we can't gather ourselves to come to the table anymore
because family gatherings are a reminder of the place
we lost our voice.

How we had to grin and bear every holiday,
but now we have a choice.

*Why do safe
spaces feel so
dangerous?*

Innocence

When they steal your innocence,
the predators move on like
nothing happened,
the world moves on like
you're a casualty of time.

But you my dear,
you stay frozen, paralyzed,
vulnerable, unprotected,
a surrendered captive
bound by your own ruminations,
a victim left to question how you
will ever walk again without your innocence.

As time moved on, it never paused to acknowledge how you
felt so useless afterward, how you wanted to die inside, how
life became so heavy.

Equations

How were we supposed to learn to love ourselves,
when our moms picked men over us,
when our molesters felt their way around our bodies,
when our dads laid hands on us,
when our teachers questioned our intelligence.

There was no love to be learned in that equation.

Tippy-Toe

In Black families, why do we tippy-toe
around the family pedophiles,
like their feelings matter more to the legacy than a Black
girl's protection?

Wedding Plans

The rapist, the married man,
the narcissist they stole parts of
you that you can never get back.

As a girl, they helped you plan
for your wedding,
but they never helped
you plan for that.

broken love

Heart Bleeds

My heart bleeds for
the Black girls
who settle
for broken love because
it's the only love they know.

Home

I spent years attempting to
fix broken lovers,
hoping to make their houses home,
they always remained houses,
sometimes even tents,
but never homes.

It took me years to realize,
the home was in me,
not them.

Audacity

You break my heart and come back,
like nothing happened,
to reconvene our regularly
scheduled program,
with no regard for your
toxicity or my humanity,
because my disregard is
our normal.

Self Esteem

Loving you feels like I left my self-esteem at home,
like I forgot to put it in my purse before I left the house,
like I dug around loose change and hard gum,
but it wasn't in its usual spot,
like I got home, and I still couldn't find it,
like I lost something that I know is in the house,
but now I have to be patient and wait for it to
reappear again when I least expect it.

Depression

Depression
feels like I'm bleeding
under my clothes.

I'm invisible until
I bleed out so much,
I can no longer hide
the blood.

Opportunity

After all the heartaches
you locked the window of
opportunity in your mind,
sealed the pain shut so tight,
that not even God himself
could pry it open.

*I hope it bruises
you the same
way you tried to
bruise me.*

Bruises

It seems like you live to
silence a black woman's voice.
I hope it bruises you
the same way you tried to bruise me.

Then you'll finally understand
what the pain feels like.

Purpose

They all served a purpose,
even if it was simply
to teach you how to
love yourself.

Courage

What he doesn't have the
courage to say with his words,
he says with his actions.

What I don't have the
courage to do with my actions,
I say with my words.

Reciprocate

I love you with my whole heart,
and still, I can't seem to get us right,
maybe if I loved you a little less,
and me a little more,
you'd reciprocate.

Needs

When my needs spilled on the
kitchen floor of our relationship,
you walked right past,
like you didn't see my mess,
left me to clean up after myself,
after all the times I cleaned up after you.

I guess in broken love,
there are no favors.

Crumbs

I thought it was me,
I spent nights ruminating,
trying to figure out why I wasn't enough,
I tried to will my way into receiving your love.

I fought so hard for your validation,
because it never occurred to me that you treat me the way
you treat yourself.

You gave me all the crumbs,
you had to offer,
and to me, they were crumbs,
but to you,
they were everything.

everyday
exhaustions

Exhaustions

Finding a therapist
who doesn't ignore
my trauma.

Finding a doctor who doesn't
dismiss my pain.

Going to the nail salon and being treated like my body
doesn't feel pain.

Daughtering parents
while simultaneously
parenting parents.

Correcting people every time they mispronounce my name.

Indulging my parents' delusions when they act like
I had a great childhood.

Peeling myself out of bed to play small for a paycheck.

Negotiating with
people and places
who don't see
my value.

Diluting myself at work to be more palatable than othered.

Expecting people to love me
more than I am willing
to love myself.

Searching my past to find my future.

Buying into the lie that the optics
of having a partner is more important than self-respect.

safe spaces

Rare Flowers

They're the rare flowers in the bunch who stand in the gap,
the ones who share their oxygen so we can breathe,
the ones who open their hearts so we can heal,
the ones who are never too consumed with their own pain
that they can't sit with us in ours,
we love them with all our hearts,
and still like the world,
we take them for granted.

Outerspace

When trauma defied gravity.

When healing appeared extraterrestrial.

When misery transcended reality.

Outside my universe,

I was welcomed onto their motherships.

Embraced in their consciousness.

Elevated into their vortex.

Centered within their orbits.

Identified by their objects.

Black girls held outer space for me.

Mustard Seeds

With made-up minds and mustard seeds of faith,
we defied conventional wisdom
and gave the status quo the middle finger,
we raised children as children,
and still simultaneously raised the bar.

When they neglected to give us a seat,
we brought a folding chair.
When we didn't want to give up our seats,
we sparked boycotts.

We, grandmothers, mothers,
 aunties, cousins,
and play cousins,
fed the whole neighborhood with just five fish and two loaves,
with hot plates and hot combs,
we burnt scalps and straightened lives.

When they enslaved us, we tapped into our superpowers
and led our people to freedom like Moses.

When they killed our sons and daughters
and incarcerated our men,
we reminded the world who mattered.

Like a rose in the middle of the concrete,

we rose from the depths of poverty,
and generations of domestics,
to birth our own narratives and our own networks.

We said "me too" first,
but it was a faint voice in the distance,
and although no one came close to hear us,
we used our victimized bodies to originate movements,
we fixed lives and baby hairs,
and transformed industries,
and beauty aisles, don't you know,
we, Black girls, are amazing!

Dignity

What we sensed,
and no one had to tell us,
the Black girls who lifted us the most,
did not carry any form of privilege.

They were family members
or women who we crossed paths with
on random days, in random places,
who filled our spirits with joy,
they drove buses, stocked shelves, cleaned toilets,
wiped butts, answered phones, waited on tables.

Yet we still beamed with pride
whenever we encountered them,
because although they carried the same burden of
dissatisfaction we all bear when we're misplaced,
they still showed up with excellence.

They taught us misplacements are no excuse for mediocrity,
because they knew their character was one of the rare
valuables that could never be stolen and sold.

They taught us dignity isn't bound in the hope
of wealth or prestige,
it's buried in the authenticity of their smiles,
the grip of their hands,

and the glow in their eyes.

Their presence reminded us,
if we're only incentivized by the world's faulty value system
to be who we are,
then we never really were in the first place.

Remember

When you see another black girl think of your sister,
not as an enemy, competitor, threat, steppingstone,
or source of shame.

Think of her as an extension of yourself,
every time you see your sister,
remember the vein of Black girlness that unites you,
and don't ever forget her.

Remember, she is worthy enough to go back and lift,
she is an extension of yourself and the reason you exist.

Remember you are the rising tide that lifts her ship,
but it only lifts when you remember not to forget.
So don't be complicit like the world that overlooks her,
the institutions and inequities that marginalize her,
the people and politics that make her hyper-visible and invisible,
or the blocks and bars that confine her,
remember not to forget,
when you soar, go back and lift her wings so she can soar too,
so that she might be reminded of her capacity to fly just like you.

Remember not to forget.
Play it softly on repeat in the back of your mind,
along with the vision of a black girl left behind.
Remember that she is simply you in reverse,

and although the world failed her,
if you fail to act, you too will inherit the curse.

So remember not to forget, remember the degrees or
hierarchy doesn't divide you as much as you think,
as you're only one paycheck or bullet
from being on her brink.

Remember you're not so distant or different,
from far away to them, we all look the same,
so it's in your best interest not to play their crabs in a bucket,
house negro, divide and conquer game.

say our names

Rain

She labors in the field of forgetfulness,
hoping her voice will be heard,
hoping her life will amount to matter,
hoping her body will be covered,
hoping her breath will be caught,
hoping her name will be remembered,
hoping her plight will be eulogized.

But there's no resting place for Black girl pain,
no water stands for the marathon.

Only rain.

Find Us

The wrong skin at the wrong time,
the pull of gravity to pools of blood,
the remorseless index fingers,
the chalk outlines,
the crying moms,
the silent witnesses,
how did it always seem to find us?

Co-parenting

Every black mom has a school picture of her son
wearing a red shirt.

She places it on her mantle
to remind her of when life was gentle,
when she and God had an explicit custody agreement in place.

When she prayed for hedges of protection,
anointed her baby boy's head with oil, and like clockwork,
she could guarantee her prized possession
would make it home safe.

A time when she and God co-parented together civilly,

when the pastor's back-to-school prayer
lasted the whole year, including holidays and summer breaks,
when her greatest worries were her son's husky clothes
and talking too much in class.

The reminder brings a tear to her eyes,
now she and God have strife
because he continues to break the custody agreement,
every time she looks up, it seems like black boys in red shirts
make it home more often to him,
than to their mommas.

Blood

Blood on hands.

Blood on seats.

Blood on walls.

Blood on streets.

Blood on schools.

Blood on sneaks.

Blood on men who do not speak.

Blood on diamonds.

Blood on ships.

Blood on hearts.

Blood on lips.

Blood on chains.

Blood on hips.

Blood on men who quickly forget.

Blood on convenience.

Blood on clout.

Blood on cages.

Blood on routes.

Blood on women.

Blood on canes.

Blood on men who do not change.

Identity

Isn't it ironic that
America's afraid to lose
her identity when she stole
it from so many others?

Perhaps what she fears most
is that she is no different than
her victims, her identity is the one
thing she will never fully own.

Sometimes the best lessons
are taught through
experience.

Survival

The ignorance
of severing the hip
and expecting the rest of the
body to survive
is the same ignorance
we exercise
when we kill our own
and expect not to die too.

Hood Cousins

Our hood cousins say
we act white because
they don't know their history.

Any strive for excellence
is white in their eyes,
but they think we're the
ones confused about
our identity.

Sell Outs

We sell our souls for designer
bags and shoes,
always the first in line,
the sell-out,
the muse,
the customer,
the tools,
the disposable,
the abused,
the impoverished,
the used.

Power

White men,
do you hoard your power
because you're afraid we'll
use our power the same way
you used yours?

Are you afraid you might be
forced to sit on the back of the bus?
That you'll endure years of generational
wealth misappropriation?

That you'll be the lowest paid and most worked in the room?
That we'll devastate your communities and redesign laws to
ensure you're the largest population in jail?

That we'll create social programs to benefit ourselves,
but the second you need help, we'll restructure them to ensure
your family receives less?

If I were you, I'd be afraid too.

Voters

Some of us want to be white
so bad that we'll vote against
our own self-interest if it means
we can have a taste of being white.

But I wonder what does white taste
like on a black self-hating tongue?

Small Minds

The small minds always blame single moms for the problems in the black community.

Contradictions

Do you ever notice the most
obvious contradictions,
like how mainstream society loves
our black culture,
and still manages to
hate our black skin?

*Our culture
is our currency.*

Culture

Our culture is our currency,
and somehow we
cheapened the value,
when we assume we
have so much of it
that we can afford to give it
away freely.

Call the Police

Call the police, on the police.

Who do we call for help on the thief,
who stole the life in disbelief,
who sowed the hate,
and dismissed the reap,
who deprived humanity,
in his defeat?

Who do we call for help for this retreat,
who recompenses,
when we cannot speak?

Before the blue became the thief,
avenger of black for his belief
black became wilted like a leaf,
seemingly prevailed his trauma relief,
white gloated, but black life's not cheap
246 years, for this we cannot speak,
stole what was never in his reach.

Who do we call for help if not the police?
The character assassin, or the real assassin?
The enemy in ghetto's bed?
The perpetuation of 13th re-read?

I'd call, but the soul is dead,
I'd cry, but bullets already to the head,
I'd say her name,
but they want me to say his instead,
I'd starve, but the lies been fed.

Who do we call for help if not the police?

When I close my eyes,
I can still hear the shrieks,
I can still see the outline of bodies,
the white sheets,
the labored faces,
the moms' weak.

Who do we call for help if not the police?

Hold on,
I'm starting to think.

Attorney Crump,
please pickup,
he can't breathe.

intersections

Civil Rights

Women of the movement remember your placement,
always behind the black man,
never adjacent,
never the center of attention,
never a statement,
never a leader amongst black men,
never equal attainment.

Decide

Even if they think they know,
they don't,
the men can't tell you where
your place is,
that's for you to decide.

Disruptors

Black Girls don't just sit there and complain,
if we're going to disrupt the status quo
we all have to support.

Pauli lit the fire,
Mahalia prompted the dream,
Fannie gathered the registrations,
Dorothy raised the height,
and Shirley brought the folding chairs.

What do you plan to contribute?

hair goals

Real Hair

How do we claim to be so real,
but the realest thing we possess,
we hide?

Lace Front

I can see the top of your lace front,
scalp realness, makeup tint,
nude cap, contrasting
against your mocha brown skin.

I wonder, do you hide for growth
or shame?

Does your head ache more from your nude cap,
or the thought of wearing your real hair?

*Don't you dare
hair shame her!*

Hair Shame

Have you ever spent a day in a black woman's head?

Have you ever had to grow back dead edges,
resuscitate a scabby chemical-burned scalp,
cut endless inches of heat-burned hair,
nurse the locs of a 4 triple C head,
witness chemotherapy dowsed hair
fall like rain on your pillow,
conceal a golfball-sized alopecia patch,
cry when the sight of grays reminds you
your egg count is low,
but your womb is still empty?

Don't you dare hair shame her,
you have no idea what she's been through.

Hair Trauma

When I say I cut my hair,
but really it fell out that way,
will you oblige me?

Will you make me feel beautiful
like a just-for-me relaxer and fresh wrap,
like a side swoop ponytail with pin curls,
like twisties with a waterfall flip,
like a vintage perm rod set,
like a double-roll updo with finger waves.

Or will you betray me?

Like all the times I changed my
hair to be accepted.

Cancerous

When did beauty become so cancerous?

What makes us beautiful on the outside,
always seems to kill us on the inside.

concrete
ceilings

Credit

Every time I speak, they repeat exactly what I say,
like my words can't be trusted.

Like they believe when they echo my sentiments,
they co-sign on my validity.

Like they have a secret language, only they understand.

That's the green light.
That's the signal.

What a black woman says is only valid
if I interject and repeat it without giving her the credit.

*Black girls
must show up
perfect.*

Glory

Black girls, you must show up perfect,
you have no room for error,
no width to grow,
no potential,
no grooming.

If they crown your head with glory in spaces you don't belong,
you have to deliver,
you have to overcompensate,
you have to commodify your worth.

These are the rules for the ones who don't belong in the first place.

Tokens

Isn't it ironic how the tokens who complain the most about
being the only ones in the room,
always lock the door behind them when no one is looking,
so other black girls can't sneak
in with their folding chairs?

Why do they think we don't notice?

gentle parenting

Therapy

If you ever questioned if you need
therapy, ask yourself,
why do belts, extension cords, and switches bring back more
childhood memories than sour patch kids, now laters, and
little debbie snacks?

When you dig deep
you always find the answer.

Rules

For your own safety,
don't sit on a man's lap,
don't walk around in towels,
keep the doors locked,
be fully clothed at all times,
don't behave fast,
be seen and not heard,
stay out of grown men's faces.

If you neglect to follow these rules,
and something happens to you,
it's your fault, and you will reap the consequences.

These are the rules.
Whether you're 4 or 24.

Problems

You beat us,
then you told us not to cry.

As if the tears were the problem.

Who cares for
the caregivers?

Caregiver

She came out of the womb bearing
the weight of the world and the pressure of the family.
As the oldest she was cautioned to stay in a child's place, and
still, they yanked her right out of position whenever a hand
was needed.

They used her paycheck to support the household,
left her responsible to care for the siblings,
disciplined her whenever the house wasn't clean.

They taught her early in life that her needs didn't matter,
stole her childhood right from under her fingertips.

Made her an adult at home way before the world left its scars.

Adulthood

My heart bleeds for the
Black girl who knows,
her adolescent intuition
doesn't lie.

No one tells her directly,
but rightly, she senses,
she is not the chosen one,
yet she must stay and endure,
because adulthood is her only
escape route.

Voids

The roundness of her face,
the wideness of her eyes,
the coarseness of her hair,
the darkness of her skin,
the thickness of her frame,
it would never be celebrated,
in the space she called home,
in the people she called family.

Invisibility

My invisibility was first validated at home.
The world only mirrored what my family showed me first.

daddy's girls

Hero

How can a monster and a
hero reside in the same body?

Why do I feel like you gave me
a childhood, and still robbed me?

Terror

When the world castrates a
Black man to remind him of his
inferiority, he becomes a terror
at home.

The wrath of his anger
sprays the whole family.

Colorful Childhood Memories

The circle of gray faces assembled at the A.A. meetings.

The cinnamon ledge where we gathered as a family
to watch the beatings.

The backseat of the blue Cavalier where
we spent hours to avoid being next.

The addicted naked brown bodies gallivanting
up and down the steps.

The white powder and jugs of neon-colored
pee around the house.

The red raging, screaming, violence
directed towards us that came out your mouth.

The real-life black trauma horror film that's hard to forgive,

The colorful childhood memories I hope to never re-live.

The colorful childhood memories I hope to never re-live.

Rage

The rage left behind more than welts,
it's the residuals I can't stand.

The flashes of trauma.

How every time I hear a man raise his voice,
I'm brought back to the powerlessness of girlhood.

The tedious walk on eggshells.

The reminder of how the whole
household lived at the mercy
of your temper.

our moms were
girls too

Boundaries

Perhaps you honored
boundaries as a girl,
but childhood taught you
there was no use in
protecting boundaries
since men always
seemed to break them
without consequence.

Teachers

We loved our mothers most because they were the first to
teach us unconditional love.

They broke our hearts,
and still came back to sew them together again.

As much as they triggered us,
still, we knew we needed them around,
still, we knew their hard lessons,
were our lessons learned,
their heartbreaks were our boundaries,
and their unrewarding self-sacrifice was our self-care.

Forgive her for being a product of her trauma.

Exposure

She was a product of her trauma,
without exposure,
she simply lived up to her normal, abuse, neglect, low expectations
what they did to her
inevitably she did to herself.

Outputs

The traumatized girl
became a controlling woman.

Fiercely judged by her outputs,
never graced for her inputs.

*Traumatized
women
are girls in
adult bodies.*

Love

The only way
I know how to love
is to stay and be abused.

I learned this type
of love from you.

Lottery

Yesterday you told me my
birthday came out straight,
and if you played you
would have won.

I watched you bet on numbers,
more than you bet on yourself,
invest more money in
the lottery system,
than you invested in your retirement.

You wrote down your plans for
when you'd hit the jackpot,
and that was the first time
I saw you write down your dreams.

I guess you thought your odds of winning the Powerball,
were better than your odds of winning in life.

Numbing

All the time you spent away from us numbing from the pain
your parents caused, would someday haunt you.

In those moments, you dug a grave of pain for your
daughters, then you'd spend your whole life trying to pay
reparations for the times you missed.

But no matter what you did to repay us, in your mind, it
would never be enough for you to forgive yourself for
Numbing.

Embarrassment

The embarrassment we felt
every time you showed up to
school in your bonnets, curlers,
work clothes, and hoopties.

Back then, we cared so much
about your appearance,
because we didn't know the
world without your presence.

If we could turn back the hands
of time, we'd cherish every
moment of embarrassment
like our last.

Food for Thought

When I was a child
you showed your
love through food:

Macaroni and Cheese
Collard Greens
Fried Chicken &
Potato Salad

I accepted it back then
because I didn't know
any better.

Now that I'm grown,
I know I needed more
than protein, saturated fats,
and carbohydrates
to fill me up,

and I know I would have starved
If it meant I could have you instead.

wound care

Black Girl Joy

Black girl joy is so uncommon when it arrives,
I treat it like stolen merchandise,
like any morsel I skim off the top
must be paid back in pain.

In my experience, joy never begat more joy,
it only served as the gray cloud right before the rain,
so when I see sightings of black girl joy,
in the PTSD of it all,
I brace myself,
hoping the next jolt of pain will be more bearable than the last.

As I heal, I try to be patient with myself
as I learn to black girl joy
free from the fear of what will happen next.

More

In this, I do declare.

You are more than the imperfections you see in the mirror.

More than the weight you gained,
more than the tiger stripes
and wrinkles that came.

More than the hair that left you,
the teeth that left you,
the womb that left you,
the breast that left you,
the sight that left you.

You are a sight.
You are more than the crumbs they left you
and the depression-filled dark nights.
You are more than the innocence they stole, and the
relationships that were
never
quite
right.

More than the bare ring finger you dawn in shame,
more than the single Black woman over 30's leftover gang.

You are more than dreams deferred
for children and men that never changed.
More than family sacrifices overlooked,
more than the time wasted and the withdraws that they took.

You are more than the eye can see, or the ear can hear,
the past can override, or respectability can bear.

So don't you dare be ashamed,
you poured from an empty cup,
and although they don't see you,
God sees you.

Keep your head up.

Luggage

Don't forget to pack your Black girl joy.

In this life,
you deserve to
carry something
other than pain.

*Black
girl tears
are real.*

Soldiers

Ask for help.

We're doing our kind a disservice
by always soldiering through.

It's one of the many reasons why everyone thinks black girl
tears aren't real.

Dumping Ground

It stops today.

You are not the
dumping ground for
everyone's trash anymore.

Lies

The worst lies are the ones we tell ourselves.
They take the longest to heal,
and they cut the deepest.

I know from experience.

Live

In this life
you died a thousand deaths,
it's time to live now.

Validation

Don't wait for them to
validate you,
validate yourself first.

Teach them how to treat you,
and if they can't follow
the lesson plan,
remove them from
the class.

Listen to black women.

Listen to Black Women

The world would be a
better place if we all
learned to listen to
black women.

Forgiveness

I forgive you most
for not seeing me.

It taught me to see myself.

Uncover

They don't make
voices like yours anymore.

So don't you dare hide.
You are the change
we need to see in this world,
but that change can
only be realized when you have
the courage to stop hiding your voice.

Don't you ever forget,
the world changes
every time a black woman
gains her courage.

Happiness

If you depend on them for happiness,
don't be surprised when life begins to feel undependable.

*It's all
working in
your favor.*

Favor

Whatever you are.
Whoever you are.
There is no mistake.

The texture of your hair.
The fullness of your lips.
The curve of your hips.
The bow of your legs.
The richness of your skin.
The pitch of your voice.

It's all here.
Working in your favor.

Unbleeding

I know you're accustomed to the bleeding,
but when it stops
accept the unbleeding too.

Embrace it with open arms
like you embraced your trauma story all these years.

Recognition

They can sleep on you all they want,
and someday they will feel the regret.
But don't you dare go through life
sleeping on yourself.

Give yourself grace for
what you were never taught.
See you, even when they don't.
Love you, even when it's hard.

You owe that to yourself.

Delusions

I died every day I lived a life beneath me.

The only thing worse than dying
was the lies I told myself
to convince me it wasn't happening.

Destiny

The parting was destined.
It forced me to find myself in the foliage,
beneath the leaves of unhappiness,
in the debris of desperation,
beyond the crawly things of loneliness,

When the fears quieted.
When the tears dried.
When the too shall passed.

I found my voice,
I honored my courage,
I learned my value.

notes for
black girls

Walk Away

Sometimes the kindest thing you can do is walk away.

Protest

The silent protest
begins when you
curate a life of exceptionalism
not solely defined by your plight.

Sacrifice

Healing doesn't come without sacrifice.

You must ask yourself,
what am I willing to sacrifice for healing?

Fine Print

Before you unpackage them, read the fine print.

Periodt

Repeat after me.

The healed me
only occupies spaces
where I'm appreciated.

Struggle Bus

Repeat after me.

I rebuke the ones who come
in the name of struggle bus love.

The love I attract is divine and
Unceasing.

Nothing is broken forever.

Nothing is Broken Forever

He pushed the lever,
lied to my face and told me I was his forever,
at a time when love was bottled, and faith was severed,
made me feel we'd always be together.

Now I see he was simply clever,
a chameleon, snake, wolf, dog, sheep, he was whatever,
I wanted him to be in my mind, but I knew better.

So many nights I cried because I hoped we'd weather,
the storm of broken dreams
but he was my never.

My never meant to be.
My never say never.
Caught in a vicious cycle,
he shattered the glass of my heart for pleasure.
However, my humpty dumpty fell,
but didn't fail forever.

God picked me and pieced me together,
I'm living proof that nothing is broken forever.
Say nothing is broken forever.

Self-care

The best form of self-care is to be your real self.

Good Ones

The good ones will let
you down too,
but still love them
anyways.

*You must
heal you.*

Limitations

If they can't heal
themselves, they can't
heal you either.

Self Love

When you get
serious about you,
they will too.

Progress

And she knew she
was healed when
everything insider her
made its way out,
when she stopped
suppressing her progress
to silence her
doubts.

Accountability

In girlhood, we have a degree of powerlessness
that must be acknowledged for healing,

In womanhood, we have a degree of accountability
that must be acknowledged for healing,

The secret is knowing where you stand.
You must heal the girl
before you can ever heal the woman.

Wisdom

If it costs you your edges,
it's not worth it.

Sometimes admitting you're
not ready to let go is the first step to letting go.

If you have to chase it,
it's not yours.

What's yours will always find you.

You don't need them to love you, to love you.

*Make space
for healing.*

Hustle

The truth is life will find you,
you will chase many hustles,
You will experience your own
version of Lemonade,
all the feels from heartbreak to forgiveness,
You will harvest the dreams of others,
labor in the field of unfulfillment,
You will dishonor your value,
compromise for their make-believe version of your worth,
You will pour from an empty cup,
normalize the pain of unrewarding self-sacrifice.

But if you're wise,
one day you will realize,
the most valuable hustle of them all
is your healing.

healing is my hustle

Acknowledgements

First and foremost, I want to thank God for equipping me with the confidence and determination to complete my first book, for teaching me to believe in the power of my voice, and for guiding me to trust your timing.

Thank you to my son Zion for believing in me and inspiring me to heal and evolve into the best version of myself. Every day you motivate me to reach outside of my comfort zone and challenge the parts of me that are broken and uncertain.

Thank you to my mother for the legacy of resilience and service you passed down to our family. I hope you feel your imprint in my work and you're filled with pride and certainty that your journey did not go unrecognized. Thank you for your reliability, for your prayers, for your humility, and for teaching me to have integrity in my work.

Thank you to my grandmother for all your sacrifice and support over the years. Your contributions helped bring me to this season in my life. Thank you Aunt Verne and Aunt Niecy for being the steady constants in my life, for filling in the gaps, and for nurturing me to evolve into the woman I am today.

And, last but not least, thank you to the everyday black girls that inspire me to heal. I pray my work empowers you to pause and reconcile your lived experiences and prioritize your healing too. In honor of our foremothers, we deserve the very best life has to offer!

DONIELLE ELIZABETH

Multi-hyphenate Donielle Elizabeth (Dawn yell) is an author, speaker, serial entrepreneur, and trailblazing black girl in tech. Donielle spent over a decade building a successful career in technology at leading Fortune 500 companies like KPMG, Deloitte, and Google. Now she's officially embarking on her writing career with her debut book, Healing is my Hustle. A curated collection of poetry inspired by Donielle's personal evolution and the lived experiences of Black women in America.

Please visit her at

DONIELLEELIZABETH.COM

or follow her on Instagram

@DONIELLE_ELIZABETH

www.ingramcontent.com/pod-product-compliance
Lightning Source LLC
Chambersburg PA
CBHW020251130626
46549CB00005B/2173